Thomas Hearne, Richard Payne Knight, Benjamin Thomas Pouncy

The landscape:

A didactic poem: in three book: addressed to Uvedale Price, Esq.

Thomas Hearne, Richard Payne Knight, Benjamin Thomas Pouncy

The landscape:
A didactic poem: in three book: addressed to Uvedale Price, Esq.

ISBN/EAN: 9783337730550

Printed in Europe, USA, Canada, Australia, Japan

Cover: Foto ©ninafisch / pixelio.de

More available books at **www.hansebooks.com**

THE

LANDSCAPE,

A

DIDACTIC POEM.

IN THREE BOOKS.

ADDRESSED TO UVEDALE PRICE, ESQ.

BY R. P. KNIGHT.

LONDON:

PRINTED BY W. BULMER AND CO.
Shakspeare Printing-Office:
AND SOLD BY G. NICOL,
PALL-MALL.

1794.

THE LANDSCAPE.

BOOK I.

How best to bid the verdant Landscape rise,
To please the fancy, and delight the eyes;
Its various parts in harmony to join
With art clandestine, and conceal'd design;
T'adorn, arrange ;—to sep'rate, and select   5
With secret skill, and counterfeit neglect;
I sing.——Do thou, O Price, the song attend ;
Instruct the poet, and assist the friend:
Teach him plain truth in numbers to express,
And shew its charms through fiction's flow'ry dress. 10
    For as the doctor's wig, and pomp of face,
Announce his knowledge of the patient's case,
And harmless drugs, roll'd in a gilded pill,
From fancy get the pow'r to cure or kill ;
So our poor palliatives may chance t'acquire   15
Some fame or favour from their gay attire ;

And learn to cure or kill that strange disease,
Which gives deformity the pow'r to please;
And shews poor Nature, shaven and defac'd,
To gratify the jaundic'd eye of taste.   20
   Whether the scene extends o'er wide domains,
Or lurks, confin'd, in low sequester'd plains;
Whether it decks the baron's gorgeous seat,
Or humbly cheers the rustic's snug retreat;
Whether it shews, from yon' high mountain's brow, 25
The water'd meads and fertile fields below;
Or, deep retir'd in solitude and shade,
It bounds its prospect to some narrow glade;
Whether it leads aloft the aching sight
To view the craggy cliff's tremendous height;   30
Or, by the murmuring riv'let's shady side,
Delights to shew the curling waters glide,
Beneath reflected rocks, or antique towers,
Amidst o'ershadowing trees, or lightly tufted flowers;
'Tis still one principle through all extends,   35
And leads through diff'rent ways to diff'rent ends.
   Whate'er its essence, or whate'er its name,
Whate'er its modes, 'tis still, in all, the same:
'Tis just congruity of parts combin'd
To please the sense, and satisfy the mind.   40

In form of limb and character of face,
We call the magic combination, *grace;*
That grace which springs from an unfetter'd mind,
Which rules the body, free and unconfin'd ;
Where native energy and native sense   45
Through ev'ry part their influence dispense ;—
In each strong feature beam ecstatic fire :
Brace ev'ry nerve and ev'ry limb inspire:—
Limbs that were never taught to move by rules,
But free alike from bandages and schools ;   50
Uncramp'd by labour hard, or dire disease,
Nor swoln by sloth, intemperance, and ease.—
Such as on Apalachean mountains stray,
And dare the panther, growling for his prey ;
Or o'er the craggy summits lightly bound,   55
And chase the deer before the panting hound.

v. 53.   It has been frequently observed by travellers, that the attitudes of savages are in general graceful and spirited ; and the great artist who now so worthily fills the President's chair in the Royal Academy, assured me, that when he first saw the Apollo of the Belvidere, he was extremely struck with its resemblance to some of the Mohawk warriors whom he had seen in America. The case is, that the Mohawks act immediately from the impulse of their minds, and know no acquired restraints or affected habits.

Or rather such as oft, in days of yore,
Display'd their vigour on Alphéus' shore;
When science, taste, and liberty combin'd
To raise the fancy and enrich the mind;   60
And each free body mov'd, without controul,
Spontaneous with the dictates of its soul.

Such were the forms which rose to Phidias' view,
When from his chisel Jove's dread image grew;
Sublimely awful, as the sov'reign god   65
Who shakes the earth's foundations with his nod;
Who bids the seasons still progressive roll,
And spread their blessings round from pole to pole;

v. 57. The state of society in Greece was such that it afforded the artist the advantages of savage, joined to those of civilized life; and in the games
and public exercises, exhibited the most perfect models of strength and agility
in men of high rank and liberal education, whose elevation of mind gave a
dignity of expression to every act and gesture of their bodies.

v. 63. The colossal statue of Jupiter, which Phidias made for the temple at Olympia, held a Sceptre in one hand, and a Victory in the other,
while the Seasons appeared to move round its head. The artist acknowledged
himself indebted for the grand expression of the countenance to the following
lines of Homer.

Η, και κυανιησιν επ' οφρυσι νευσε Κρονιων·
Αμβροσιαι δ'αρα χαιται επερρωσαντο ανακτος,
Κρατος απ' αθανατοιο· μεγαν δ'ελελιξεν Ολυμπον.   IL. A. 528.

Such too the Sicyonian sculptor taught
To model motion, and imbody thought;   70

v. 69. Lysippus of Sicyon added the last refinements of elegance to the
art of sculpture. He observed that *the old statuaries made men as they were,
and he, as they seemed to be.* (ab illis factos, quales essent, homines: a se, quales
viderentur esse. Plin. l. xxxiv. c. 19.) It is much to be regretted that
we have not the original Greek of this curious and singular expression extant; as it is somewhat equivocally, and, probably, imperfectly recorded
in the concise Latin of Pliny; who scarcely knew enough of art to feel
its force, or comprehend its meaning. The great artist appears to have
been so thoroughly master of the human frame, that he could represent
all its actions and positions in *the abstract*; without referring to individual
models; and thus to allow for the errors of vision, and the difference between
real and *visible* perspective; or rather, the difference of perspective in objects
as they appear to the eye only, and as they appear to the eye corrected by the
understanding. This difference may at any time be discovered and ascer-
tained, by tracing a figure, with projecting parts, through a plate of glass,
or other transparent substance. In such a traced drawing, the lineal perspective must necessarily be correct; but nevertheless the projections will
become much larger in it, than they appear to the eye in the object from
which it was taken; because the mind, knowing their real size from the
evidence of another sense, corrects the sight in a manner so habitually in-
stantaneous, as to be quite imperceptible. Hence some degree of real in-
correctness is always necessary to produce apparent precision; and as
the Greek artists worked much less mechanically than the moderns, they
were the more likely to sacrifice the means to the end. All their finest efforts
were employed in representing those momentary actions and expressions,

Pure abstract beauty's fleeting shades to trace,
And fix the image of ideal grace:
Combining what he felt with what he saw ;
And penetrating nature's inmost law:
To no one single model stiffly bound,   75
But boldly ranging all creation round,
He made his breathing figures light and free,
Not as men were, but as they seem'd to be.

  Curse on the pedant jargon, that defines
Beauty's unbounded forms to given lines !   80
With scorn eternal mark the cautious fool,
Who dares not judge till he consults his rule !
Who, when strong passions shake the actor's frame,
And all his soul has catch'd the Poet's flame,

for which no stationary model could be found ; wherefore they were obliged
to work as much from their minds, as their eyes; and to employ such means
as were most certain of producing the intended effects, without considering
whether or not they were precisely the same as those which nature employs
to produce such effects. Hence in some of the finest specimens of art now
extant (particularly the Apollo of the Belvidere) partial inaccuracies, even
when apparent, contribute to the general correctness of the action and expression. This was probably the case with the works of Lysippus; and
may account for the remark above cited, which an artist of his fire would
naturally think a sufficient answer to the impertinent observations of those
critics, who measured his works, instead of looking at them.

Thinks but of rhetoric's phlegmatic laws,   85
And with his stop-watch measures ev'ry pause :
Or when, Salvator, from thy daring hand
Appears, in burnish'd arms, some savage band,—
Each figure boldly pressing into life,
And breathing blood, calamity, and strife ;   90
Should coldly measure each component part,
And judge thy genius by a surgeon's art :
Or else, where Rembrandt, through some darken'd room,
Spreads his soft tints, and animates the gloom,
Refuse t'admire the sweetly blended light,   95
Till some optician had pronounc'd it right.
   Such formal coxcombs let us still defy,
And dare be pleas'd, although we know not why.
Not that I'd check the careful student's toil ;
For culture's needful to the happiest soil :   100
All art, by labour, slowly is acquired ;—
The madman only fancies 'tis inspired.
The vain, rash upstart, thinks he can create,
Ere yet his hand has learn'd to imitate ;
While senseless dash and random flourish try   105
The place of skill and freedom to supply.
But when the master's hand, in wanton play,
Presumes beyond precision's bounds to stray,

Light, bold, and steady, as his pencil flies,
Small partial errors sink before our eyes: 110
His glowing touch, elastic, strong, and free,
Still shews us Nature *as she seems to be;*
And with expression, just in ev'ry part,
Appeals from sense directly to the heart.

   E'en forms of molten brass, and sculptur'd stone 115
Have learn'd this magic pow'r of art to own;
For though the sculptor's hand advances slow,
And no free touches from the chisel flow;
Yet science, led by genius, has supplied
What Nature's self appear'd to have denied.   120

   When sudden poisons freeze Laocoon's veins,
The skin seems curdled with convulsive pains;

---

v. 111.   See note on v. 69.

v. 121.   The group of Laocoon and his sons, in the Cortile of the Belvidere, is the work of Agesander, Polidorus, and Athenodorus of Rhodes;
and is mentioned by Pliny as the most consummate piece of art extant in
his time (opus omnibus et picturæ et statuariæ artis præponendum. Lib.
xxxvi. c. 4.) Happily the surface is perfectly preserved: otherwise the
excellence here alluded to would have been lost.

   Virgil has evidently taken his description of the death of Laocoon from
this group; but he has grossly misunderstood, and miserably debased the
sublime ideas of the Greek sculptors, in making the suffering hero roar out,
when bitten by the serpent, as a bull roars when stricken by the sacrificer.

The nerves contracted, e'en in marble rise,
And the last rays seem quiv'ring in his eyes:
Yet view the wonder with attention near,   125
And the rough touches of the tool appear
Impress'd with seeming ease and bold neglect,
But plac'd with care, and labour'd for effect.

    When Delphi's god advances o'er the plain,
And views, triumphant, the dire serpent slain;   130
Though symmetry in parts neglected lies,
The whole displays the godhead to our eyes;
Lightly th'elastic marble seems to tread,
And trace th' unerring shaft his hand has sped:
While scorn celestial rises in his face,   135
Attemper'd sweet, with more than mortal grace;

> Clamores simul horrendos ad sidera tollit;
> Qualis mugitus, fugit quum saucius aram
> Taurus.——   Æn. ii. 222.

In the marble, the breast is expanded, and the throat contracted, to shew that the agonies which convulse the frame are borne in silence.

v. 129. In the statue of Apollo, in the same Cortile of the Belvidere, the left shoulder, which is raised, is farther from the neck than the right, which is fallen. An inaccuracy so gross, in a work of such masterly excellence, must have been intended; and, I believe, the wonderful expression of lightness, movement, and agility, which distinguishes this figure, is considerably augmented by it.

From ev'ry sordid, earthly passion free,
And feeling only as a deity.

In humbler art the self same laws obtain:
Nature in all rejects the pedant's chain;   140
Which binding beauty in its waving line,
Destroys the charm it vainly would define;
For nature still irregular and free,
Acts not by lines, but gen'ral sympathy.
The path that moves in even serpentine,   145
Is still less nat'ral than the pointed line:
When o'er the level lawn you chance to stray,
Nature and taste direct the nearest way;
But when you traverse rough uneven ground,
Consult your ease, and you will oft go round: 150
The best of rules are those of common use;
Affected taste is but refin'd abuse.

First fix the points to which you wish to go;
Then let your easy path spontaneous flow;
With no affected turn or artful bend,   155
To lead you round still farther from the end:
For, as the principle of taste is sense,
Whate'er is void of meaning gives offence.

 " But in your grand approach," the critic cries,
" Magnificence requires some sacrifice:— 160

 v. 159. That I may not be suppossd to deal unfairly with the modern

" As you advance unto the palace gate,
" Each object should announce the owner's state ;
" His vast possessions, and his wide domains ;
" His waving woods, and rich unbounded plains."
He, therefore, leads you many a tedious round,   165
To shew th'extent of his employer's ground ;
Climbs o'er the hills, and to the vales descends ;
Then mounts again, through lawn that never ends.

    But why not rather, at the porter's gate,
Hang up the map of all my lord's estate,   170
Than give his hungry visiters the pain
To wander o'er so many miles in vain?

improvers of places, or landscape gardeners, I must inform the reader, that I
have taken this passage from one, who will be readily and universally al-
lowed to be the most skilful and eminent among them. Mr. Repton, in
his plan for improving Tatton park, in Cheshire, with which he means
to favour the public in the general collection of his works, and in which
he has professedly detailed the principles of his art, suggests many expe-
dients for shewing the extent of property, and among others, that of
placing the family arms upon the neighbouring mile-stones; but as diffi-
culties might arise among the trustees of the turnpikes, who might each
wish to have his own arms on some particular stone, I flatter myself that the
more direct and explicit means of gratifying purse-proud vanity which I here
propose, may not be thought unworthy of the attention of those improvers,
who make this gratification the object of their labours.

For well we know this sacrifice is made,
Not to his taste, but to his vain parade;
And all it does, is but to shew combin'd   175
His wealth in land, and poverty in mind.
   The best approach to ev'ry beauteous scene,
Is where it's least expected or foreseen;
Where nought occurs t'anticipate surprise,
Or bring the Landscape piecemeal to the eyes: 180
For as bright tints of yellow, blue, or red,
In gay confusion o'er the pallet spread,
May please the infant; but until combin'd,
Afford no pleasure to th'experienc'd mind;
So beauteous objects, unconnected seen,   185
Where wide blank spaces ever intervene,
Materials for the Landscape may supply,
And, dazzling, please the rude unskilful eye;
Which wild variety with zeal pursues,
And still is pleased the more, the more it views: 190
But cautiously will taste its stores reveal;
Its greatest art is aptly to conceal;
To lead, with secret guile, the prying sight
To where component parts may best unite,
And form one beauteous, nicely blended whole,   195
To charm the eye and captivate the soul.

As he who shines supreme in ev'ry art,
That guides the taste, or elevates the heart;
Whose genius, like the sun, serenely bright,
From unknown sources beams eternal light;   200
And though successive ages roll away,
Systems on systems triumph and decay,
Empires on empires in oblivion fall,
And ruin spread alternate over all;
Still lives unclouded in perpetual day,   205
And darts through realms unborn his intellectual ray:
As he, in plain undecorated lines,
Just hints the subject of his vast designs;
But leaves the mighty scenes that crowd behind
To rush at once upon the hearer's mind: 210
So let th' approach and entrance to your place
Display no glitter, and affect no grace;
But still in careless easy curves proceed,
Through the rough thicket or the flow'ry mead;

v. 197. The unadorned simplicity with which Homer begins his poems, has been always so universally admired, that I wonder it has not been imitated in all other works of taste and genius. In building, and what is called landscape gardening, it has not only been neglected, but studiously avoided; though, in reality, more important in augmenting the effect, and progressively interesting the attention, than in poetry.

14

Till bursting from some deep-imbower'd shade, 215
Some narrow valley, or some op'ning glade,
Well mix'd and blended in the scene, you shew
The stately mansion rising to the view.
But mix'd and blended, ever let it be
A mere component part of what you see. 220
For if in solitary pride it stand,
'Tis but a lump, encumbering the land,
A load of inert matter, cold and dead,
Th' excrescence of the lawns that round it spread.

    Component parts in all the eye requires: 225
One formal mass for ever palls and tires.
To make the Landscape grateful to the sight,
Three points of distance always should unite;
And howsoe'er the view may be confin'd,
Three mark'd divisions we shall always find: 230
Not more, where Claude extends his prospect wide,
O'er Rome's Campania to the Tyrrhene tide,
(Where tow'rs and temples, mould'ring to decay,
In pearly air appear to die away,

v. 215, and 221. Compare the same scene in plates I. and II.; in the latter dressed in the modern style, and in the former, undressed. That my representation of the effects of both may be perfectly fair, I have chosen the commonest English scenery.

And the soft distance, melting from the eye,   235
Dissolves its forms into the azure sky),
Than where, confin'd to some sequester'd rill,
Meek Hobbima presents the village mill:—
Not more, where great Salvator's mountains rise,
And hide their craggy summits in the skies;   240
While tow'ring clouds in whirling eddies roll,
And bursting thunders seem to shake the pole;
Than in the ivy'd cottage of Ostade,
Waterloe's copse, or Rysdael's low cascade.
    Though oft o'erlook'd, the parts which are most near
Are ever found of most importance here;   246
For though in nature oft the wand'ring eye
Roams to the distant fields, and skirts the sky,
Where curiosity its look invites,
And space, not beauty, spreads out its delights;   250
Yet in the picture all delusions fly,
And nature's genuine charms we there descry;
The composition rang'd in order true,
Brings every object fairly to the view;
And, as the field of vision is confin'd,   255
Shews all its parts collected to the mind.
    Hence let us learn, in real scenes, to trace
The true ingredients of the painter's grace;

To lop redundant parts, the coarse refine,
Open the crowded, and the scanty join.   260
But, ah! in vain:—See yon fantastic band,
With charts, pedometers, and rules in hand,
Advance triumphant, and alike lay waste
The forms of nature, and the works of taste!
T'improve, adorn, and polish, they profess;   265
But shave the goddess, whom they come to dress;
Level each broken bank and shaggy mound,
And fashion all to one unvaried round;
One even round, that ever gently flows,
Nor forms abrupt, nor broken colours knows;   270
But, wrapt all o'er in everlasting green,
Makes one dull, vapid, smooth, and tranquil scene.

   Arise, great poet, and again deplore
The fav'rite reeds that deck'd thy Mincius' shore!
Protect the branches, that in Hæmus shed   275
Their grateful shadows o'er thy aching head;

---

v. 273.   ——Tardis ubi ingens flexibus errat
        Mincius, et tenerâ prætexit arundine ripas. VIRG. GEORG. iii. 14.
    See also the 1st Bucolick, where Virgil so pathetically laments the con-
fiscation and distribution among the soldiery of the estates in that country.
    v. 275.   ——O qui me gelidis in vallibus Hæmi
        Sistat, et ingenti ramorum protegat umbrâ.

Shav'd to the brink, our brooks are taught to flow
Where no obtruding leaves or branches grow ;
While clumps of shrubs bespot each winding vale,
Open alike to ev'ry gleam and gale ;   280
Each secret haunt, and deep recess display'd,
And intricacy banish'd with its shade.

   Hence, hence ! thou haggard fiend, however call'd,
Thin, meagre genius of the bare and bald ;
Thy spade and mattock here at length lay down,   285
And follow to the tomb thy fav'rite Brown :
Thy fav'rite Brown, whose innovating hand
First dealt thy curses o'er this fertile land ;
First taught the walk in formal spires to move,
And from their haunts the secret Dryads drove ;   290
With clumps bespotted o'er the mountain's side,
And bade the stream 'twixt banks close shaven glide ;
Banish'd the thickets of high-bow'ring wood,
Which hung, reflected, o'er the glassy flood ;
Where screen'd and shelter'd from the heats of day,
Oft on the moss-grown stone repos'd I lay,   296

v. 277. See plate I. in the middle distance, a brook flowing in its natural
banks; and in plate II. the same brook, with its banks dressed by an
improver.

And tranquil view'd the limpid stream below,
Brown with o'erhanging shade, in circling eddies flow.
　Dear peaceful scenes, that now prevail no more,
Your loss shall ev'ry weeping muse deplore!　　300
Your poet, too, in one dear favour'd spot,
Shall shew your beauties are not quite forgot;
Protect from all the sacrilegious waste
Of false improvement, and pretended taste,
One tranquil vale; where oft, from care retir'd,　　305
He courts the muse, and thinks himself inspir'd;
Lulls busy thought and rising hope to rest,
And checks each wish that dares his peace molest.
　Hence, proud ambition's vain delusive joys!
Hence, worldly wisdom's solemn empty toys!　　310
Let others seek the senate's loud applause,
And, glorious, triumph in their country's cause!
Let others, bravely prodigal of breath,
Go grasp at honour in the jaws of death;—
Their toils may everlasting glories crown,　　315
And Heaven record their virtues with its own!
　Let me, retir'd from bus'ness, toil, and strife,
Close amidst books and solitude my life;
Beneath yon high-brow'd rocks in thickets rove,
Or, meditating, wander through the grove;　　320

Or, from the cavern, view the noontide beam
Dance on the rippling of the lucid stream,
While the wild woodbine dangles o'er my head,
And various flowers around their fragrance spread;
Or where, 'midst scatter'd trees, the op'ning glade   325
Admits the well-mix'd tints of light and shade;
And as the day's bright colours fade away,
Just shews my devious solitary way:
While thick'ning glooms around are slowly spread,
And glimm'ring sun-beams gild the mountain's head:
Then homeward as I saunt'ring move along,   331
The nightingale begins his ev'ning song;
Chaunting a requiem to departed light,
That smooths the raven down of sable night.

    When morning's orient beams again arise,   335
And the day reddens in the eastern skies;
I hear the cawing rooks salute the dawn,
High in the oaks which overhang the lawn:
Perch'd up aloft, the council sits in state,
And the grove echoes with their loud debate;   340
While various ways th'advent'rous squadrons fly,
Explore the thickets, and the fallows try;
Dig up the earth-worms, wrapt in spiry folds,
And drag the embryo beetles from their holds;

v. 343.   The farmers, when they see the rooks feeding on the fields that

Till tir'd with toil, and satiated with prey,   345
Again they homeward bend their airy way;
And boastful celebrate, in clamours loud,
Their various triumphs to th' attending crowd.
   Yet e'en these little politicians know
The ills, that from a social compact flow ;—   350
Oft have I seen their guardian trusts betray'd,
And pilf'ring thieves the wand'rer's nest invade;
Tear down the long result of all his toil,
And build their mansions with their neighbour's spoil;
Till hosts of friends, assembling in his cause,   355
Drive off the plund'rers, and assert the laws;
Whence parties rise, and factions kindle round,
And wars and tumults through the wood resound.
   Here, while I view their feuds of petty strife,
I learn, unfelt, the ills of public life;   360
And see well acted, in their little state,
All that ambition aims at in the great.

are newly sown, are apt to imagine that they are eating the seed-corn, and thence endeavour to destroy them; whereas they are in reality digging up the worms and slugs, and by that means doing the most essential service. The large white grub with a brown head, which, after lying three years in the ground, becomes the common brown beetle or caterpillar, and which is so destructive to the roots of grass and corn, while in this embryo state, is a favourite food with them;—whence those insects seldom appear near to rookeries.

Hail! happy scenes of contemplative ease,
Where pleasure's sense, and wisdom is to please:—
Not such as, in the past'ral poet's strains,   365
Fancy spreads o'er imaginary plains;
Where love-sick shepherds, sillier than their sheep,
In love-sick numbers, full as silly, weep;
But such as nature's common charms produce
For social man's delight and common use;   370
Form'd to amuse, instruct, and please the mind,
By study polish'd, and by arts refin'd;
Arts, whose benignant powers around dispense
The grace of pleasure, that's approv'd by sense;
And, bending nature to their soft controul,   375
Expand, exalt, and purify the soul.
   The monk, secluded by his early vow,
The blessings of retreat can never know:
Barren of facts and images, his mind
Can no materials for reflection find;   380
Dark rankling passions on his temper prey,
And drive each finer sentiment away;
Breed foul desires; and in his heart foment
The secret germs of lurking discontent:
Long weary days and nights successive roll,   385
And no bright vision dawns upon his soul;

No gleams of past delight can mem'ry bring,
To stimulate the flight of fancy's wing:
In vain, to distant Hope, Religion calls,
When dark vacuity his mind appalls:—   390
Without, a dismal sameness reigns around;
Within, a dreary void is only found.
     From mere privation nothing can proceed,
Nor can the mind digest unless it feed;
For understanding, like the body, grows   395
From food, from exercise, and due repose;
Nor is it nourish'd, by repeating o'er
What others have repeated oft before;
Study but methodizes and corrects
What observation previously collects: 400
Train'd by experience, nurtur'd by retreat,
Reason makes theory and practice meet;
And onward still, as daring thoughts pursue
The chain of being, stretch'd from mortal view,
Bids every passion yield to its controul,   405
And calm contentment beam upon the soul;
Shews what we are, and all that we can be,
And makes us feel, that all is vanity.

THE LANDSCAPE.

BOOK II.

OFT when I've seen some lonely mansion stand,
Fresh from th' improver's desolating hand,
'Midst shaven lawns, that far around it creep
In one eternal undulating sweep;
And scatter'd clumps, that nod at one another,   5
Each stiffly waving to its formal brother;
Tir'd with th' extensive scene, so dull and bare,
To Heav'n devoutly I've address'd my pray'r,—
Again the moss-grown terraces to raise,
And spread the labyrinth's perplexing maze;   10
Replace in even lines the ductile yew,
And plant again the ancient avenue.
Some features then, at least, we should obtain,
To mark this flat, insipid, waving plain;

v. 13.   See plate I.—In the distance, a mansion-house with the ancient
decorations; and in plate II. the same modernized.

Some vary'd tints and forms would intervene,   15
To break this uniform, eternal green.
   E'en the trimm'd hedges, that inclos'd the field,
Some consolation to the eye might yield;
But even these are studiously remov'd,
And clumps and bareness only are approv'd.   20
Though the old system against nature stood,
At least in this, 'twas negatively good:—
Inclos'd by walls, and terraces, and mounds,
Its mischiefs were confin'd to narrow bounds;
Just round the house, in formal angles trac'd,   25
It mov'd responsive to the builder's taste;
Walls answer'd walls, and alleys, long and thin,
Mimick'd the endless passages within.
   But kings of yew, and goddesses of lead,
Could never far their baneful influence spread;   30
Coop'd in the garden's safe and narrow bounds,
They never dar'd invade the open grounds;
Where still the roving ox, or browsing deer,
From such prim despots kept the country clear;
While uncorrupted still, on every side,   35
The ancient forest rose in savage pride;
And in its native dignity display'd
Each hanging wood and ever verdant glade;

Where ev'ry shaggy shrub and spreading tree
Proclaim'd the seat of native liberty ;   40
In loose and vary'd groups unheeded thrown,
And never taught the planter's care to own:
Some, tow'ring upwards, spread their arms in state ;
And others, bending low, appear'd to wait:
While scatter'd thorns, brows'd by the goat and deer,
Rose all around, and let no lines appear.   46

    Such groups did Claude's light pencil often trace,
The foreground of some classic scene to grace ;
Such, humble Waterloe, to nature true,
Beside the copse, or village pasture drew.

    But ah ! how diff'rent is the formal lump
Which the improver plants, and calls a clump!
Break, break, ye nymphs, the fence that guards it round!
With browsing cattle, all its forms confound!
As chance or fate will have it, let it grow ;—   55
Here spiring high ;—there cut, or trampled low.
No apter ornament can taste provide
T' embellish beauty, or defect to hide ;

v. 47.   See plate I. in the foreground.

v. 51.   See plate II. a clump substituted to the group in the preceding plate.

If train'd with care and undiscover'd skill,
Its just department in the scene to fill ;   60
But with reserve and caution be it seen,
Nor e'er surrounded by the shaven green ;
But in the foreground boldly let it rise,
Or join'd with other features meet the eyes:
The distant mansion, seen beneath its shade,   65
Is often advantageously display'd :—
But here, once more, ye rural muses, weep
The ivy'd balustrades, and terrace steep ;
Walls, mellow'd into harmony by time,
O'er which fantastic creepers us'd to climb ;   70
While statues, labyrinths, and alleys, pent
Within their bounds, at least were innocent !
Our modern taste, alas ! no limit knows :—
O'er hill, o'er dale, through woods and fields it flows ;
Spreading o'er all its unprolific spawn,   75
In never-ending sheets of vapid lawn.
  True composition all extremes rejects,
And just proportions still, of all, selects ;

v. 65. See plate I.
  v. 67. See plates I. and II. the same house with and without these old-
fashioned decorations.

Wood, water, lawn, in just gradation joins,
And each with artful negligence combines: 80
But still in level, or slow-rising ground,
The wood should always form th' exterior bound;
Not as a belt, encircling the domain,
Which the tir'd eye attempts to trace in vain;
But as a bolder outline to the scene   85
Than the unbroken turf's smooth even green.
But if some distant hill o'er all arise,
And mix its azure colours with the skies;
Or some near mountain its rough summits shew,
And bound with broken crags the Alpine view;   90
Or rise, with even slope and gradual swell,
Like the broad cone, or wide-extended bell;—
Never attempt, presumptuous, to o'erspread
With starv'd plantations its bleak, barren head:
Nature herself the rash design withstands,   95
And guards her wilds from innovating hands;
Which, if successful, only would disgrace
Her giant limbs with fripp'ry, fringe, and lace.

v. 83.   The belt with which Mr. Brown and his followers encircled the
scenes of their improvements, is a boundary only in the map.   In nature,
the highest, and not the most distant parts of the demesnes, are the boundaries
to the different stages of distance.

Whatever foremost glitters to the eye,
Should near the middle of the Landscape lie ;—   100
Such as the stagnant pool, or rippling stream,
That foams and sparkles in the sun's bright beam ;
Not to attract th' unskilful gazer's sight,
But to concentrate, and disperse the light ;
To shew the clear reflection of the day,   105
And dart through hanging trees the refluent ray ;
Where semi-lights with semi-shadows join,
And quiv'ring play in harmony divine.
Motion and life the thicket seems to take,
And then reflect them back upon the lake :   110
Soft flick'ring tints in every part appear,
Bright without glare, without distinction clear ;
While the strong lights that in the centre play,

v. 105, &c.   These beautiful effects of the sun shining through trees that
overhang water, have rarely been attended to by artists; and never attempted
to be imitated by any, that I know of, except Claude.   The practice of our
students in Landscape-painting, in making only slight sketches from nature,
and finishing them at home, must effectually prevent their excelling in that
art; which consists in the power of imitating colours rather than forms.   If
they were to make their designs at home, and put in the light and shade and
colouring from nature, their course of study would be much more reasonable
and profitable.

As more diverged spread a fainter ray,
Till lost in thick'ning shades they die away.　　115
　Although your waters be of small extent,
And 'midst high banks and shadowy thickets pent,
Look not with envy at the boundless meer,
That spreads o'er miles, from all incumbrance clear;
Nor think the vast Maragnon's rolling tide,　　120
When rivers numberless have swell'd his pride,
Displays to heav'n so beautiful a stream,
As the wide-wand'ring Wye, or rapid Team:—
Nor yet expect, where Niagara roars,
And stuns the nations round Ontario's shores,　　125
To find such true sublimity display'd,
As in rich Tibur's broken, wild cascade.
　Oft have I heard the silly trav'ller boast
The grandeur of Ontario's endless coast;
Where, far as he could dart his wand'ring eye,　　130
He nought but boundless water could descry.
　With equal reason, Keswick's favour'd pool
Is made the theme of ev'ry wond'ring fool;
With bogs and barrenness here compass'd round,
With square inclosures there, and fallow'd ground;　135
O'er its deep waves no promontories tower,
No lofty trees, high over-arch'd, imbower;

No winding creek or solitary bay,
'Midst pendant rocks or woods is seen to stray:
But small prim islands, with blue fir-trees crown'd, 140
Spread their cold shadows regularly round;
Whilst over all vast crumbling mountains rise,
Mean in their forms, though of gigantic size.
    Ah! what avails the mountain's dizzy height,
Or base that far extends beyond the sight; 145
If flat, dull, shapes behind each other rise,
And fritter'd outlines cut against the skies?
'Tis form, not magnitude, adorns the scene;—
A hillock may be grand, and the vast Andes mean.
    But as vain painters, destitute of skill, 150
Large sheets of canvas with large figures fill,
And think with shapes gigantic to supply
Grandeur of form, and grace of symmetry:—
So the rude gazer ever thinks to find
The view sublime, where vast and unconfin'd. 155
    'Tis not the giant of unwieldy size,
Piling up hills on hills to scale the skies,
That gives an image of the true sublime,
Or the best subject for the lofty rhyme;
But nature's common works, by genius dress'd, 160
With art selected, and with taste express'd;

Where sympathy with terror is combin'd,
To move, to melt, and elevate the mind.

    Still less, in common objects of the sense,
Can we with symmetry of form dispense:—   165
The lake or river should not be so wide
As not to shew distinctly either side;
Unless remote, in hazy distance seen,
It dimly glimmers through the azure scene:
Nor should the mountain lift so high its head,   170
Or its circumference so widely spread,
As each approaching object to o'erpower,
Shame the high-spreading oak, or lofty tower;
And, by reducing ev'ry feature round,
Poor Lilliput with Brobdignag confound.   175
    To shew the nice embellishments of art,
The foreground ever is the properest part;
For e'en minute and trifling objects near,
Will grow important, and distinct appear:
No leaf of fern, low weed, or creeping thorn,   180
But, near the eye, the Landscape may adorn;
Either when tufted o'er the moss-grown stone,
Or down the slope in loose disorder thrown;

---

v. 180.   See plate I. the bank in the foreground.

Or, richly spread along the level green,
It breaks the tints and variegates the scene.   185
 . But here again, ye rural nymphs, oppose
Nature's and Art's confederated foes!
Break their fell scythes, that would these beauties shave,
And sink their iron rollers in the wave!
Your favourite plants, and native haunts protect,   190
In wild obscurity, and rude neglect;
Or teach proud man his labour to employ
To form and decorate, and not destroy;
Teach him to place, and not remove the stone
On yonder bank, with moss and fern o'ergrown;   195
To cherish, not mow down, the weeds that creep
Along the shore, or overhang the steep;
To break, not level, the slow-rising ground,
And guard, not cut, the fern that shades it round.
   The cover'd seat, that shelters from the storm,   200
May oft a feature in the Landscape form;
Whether compos'd of native stumps and roots,
It spreads the creeper's rich fantastic shoots;
Or, rais'd with stones, irregularly pil'd,
It seems some cavern, desolate and wild: 205

v. 185.   See plate II. the same bank dressed and levelled in the style of modern taste.

But still of dress and ornament beware ;
And hide each formal trace of art with care :
Let clust'ring ivy o'er its sides be spread,
And moss and weeds grow scatter'd o'er its head.

  The stately arch, high-rais'd with massive stone ;
The pond'rous flag, that forms a bridge alone ;   211
The prostrate tree, or rudely propt-up beam,
That leads the path across the foaming stream ;
May each the scene with diff'rent beauty grace,
If shewn with judgment in its proper place.   215
But false refinement vainly strives to please,
With the thin, fragile bridge of the Chinese ;
Light and fantastical, yet stiff and prim,
The child of barren fancy turn'd to whim :
Whim ! whose extravagancies ever try   220
The vacancies of fancy to supply :
And as the coward, when his passions rave,
Rushes on dangers that appall the brave ;

---

v. 212. See plate I. In the middle distance, a view of a rustic bridge, taken from one that I have erected.—For the various effects of different arched and flagged bridges, see the Liber Veritatis of Claude ; in which some of almost every form are introduced, in every kind of situation.

217. See plate II. a Chinese bridge substituted to the preceding rustic one.

So frigid whim beyond invention flies,
O'erleaps congruity, and sense defies;   225
Imagines cities in sequester'd bowers,
And floods their streets with artificial showers:
With fairs and markets crowds a garden's glades,
And turns the fishwomen to Tartar maids;
Bids gibbets rise, and rotting felons swing,   230
To deck the prospects of a pious king;
And in low filth, which foul disgust excites,
Finds the sublime, which awes and yet delights.

    The quarry long neglected, and o'ergrown
With thorns, that hang o'er mould'ring beds of stone,
May oft the place of nat'ral rocks supply,   236
And frame the verdant picture to the eye;

v. 226. See a Treatise on Oriental Gardening, by Sir W. Chambers; in which all these happy conceits are seriously attributed to the Emperor of China, and stated as the highest efforts of taste which European monarchs can pretend to imitate. Atque utinam his potius nugis tota illa dedisset—tempora—his amusement would at least have been innocent; and the wealth of an exhausted nation might have escaped from being squandered in erecting buildings which tumble down before they are finished; and which, after the expence of near half a million, are found to be too weak and fragile to sustain even a plaster cast of a large statue; the Royal Academy having lately been obliged to reject one of the Farnese Hercules, because they have no room above ground strong enough to support it.

Or, closing round the solitary seat,
Charm with the simple scene of calm retreat.

 Large stems of trees, and branches spreading wide,
May oft adorn the scenes which they divide;   241
For pond'rous masses, and deep shadows near,
Will shew the distant scene more bright and clear;
And forms distinctly mark'd, at once supply
A scale of magnitude and harmony;   245
From which receding gradually away,
The tints grow fainter and the lines decay.

 The same effects may also be display'd
Through the high vaulted arch or colonnade :—
But harsh and cold the builder's work appears,   250
Till soften'd down by long revolving years;
Till time and weather have conjointly spread
Their mould'ring hues and mosses o'er its head.

 Bless'd is the man, in whose sequester'd glade,
Some ancient abbey's walls diffuse their shade;   255
With mould'ring windows pierc'd, and turrets crown'd,
And pinnacles with clinging ivy bound.

---

v. 240. Almost all the great landscape-painters have employed this means of producing effect; so that to point out particular instances would be superfluous. The Liber Veritatis has many.

Bless'd too is he, who, 'midst his tufted trees,
Some ruin'd castle's lofty towers sees;
Imbosom'd high upon the mountain's brow,   260
Or nodding o'er the stream that glides below.
   Nor yet unenvy'd, to whose humbler lot
Falls the retir'd and antiquated cot;—
Its roof with weeds and mosses cover'd o'er,
And honeysuckles climbing round the door;   265
While mantling vines along its walls are spread,
And clust'ring ivy decks the chimney's head.
   Still happier he (if conscious of his prize)
Who sees some temple's broken columns rise,
'Midst sculptur'd fragments, shiver'd by their fall, 270
And tott'ring remnants of its marble wall;—
Where ev'ry beauty of correct design,
And vary'd elegance of art, combine
With nature's softest tints, matur'd by time,
And the warm influence of a genial clime.   275
   But let no servile copiest appear,
To plant his paltry imitations here;
To shew poor Baalbec dwindled to the eye,
And Pæstum's fanes with columns six feet high!
With urns and cenotaphs our vallies fill,   280
And bristle o'er with obelisks the hill!

Such buildings English nature must reject,
And claim from art th' appearance of neglect:
No decoration should we introduce,
That has not first been nat'raliz'd by use;   285
And at the present, or some distant time,
Become familiar to the soil and clime:
For as the cunning nymph, with giddy care
And wanton wiles, conceals her study'd air;
And each acquired grace of fashion tries   290
To hide in nature's negligent disguise;
While with unseen design and cover'd art
She charms the sense, and plays around the heart:
So ev'ry pleasing object more will please,
As less th' observer its intention sees;   295
But thinks it form'd for use, and plac'd by chance
Within the limits of his transient glance.
But no jackdaw, in borrow'd plumage gay,
Nor sooty sweeper, on the first of May,
With powder'd periwig, and raddled face,   300
And tatter'd garment, trimm'd with paper lace,
Can more the bounds of common sense trangress
In tawdry incongruity of dress,
Than rural cockneys, when they vainly try
To deck, like village fanes, the barn or sty;   305

And o'er the dunghill's litter'd filth and mire,
Show the gilt pinnacle or whiten'd spire:—
Doubly disgusted, such poor tricks we see,
That even counterfeit deformity!

O happy days, when art to nature true,   310
No tricks of dress, or whims of fashion knew!
Ere forms fantastical, or prim grimace
Had dar'd usurp the honour'd name of grace;
When taste was sense, embellish'd and refin'd
By fancy's charms, and reason's force combin'd;   315

v. 310, &c.   The uniform principle of grace and elegance which prevailed in all the works of Greece and her colonies, through such a vast variety of states, differing in climate, manners, laws, and governments, has
been observed by antiquaries as one of the most extraordinary phænomena
in the history of man.   The beautiful, and yet varied forms of the earthen
funereal vases, which are called Etruscan, though principally of Greek ma-
nufacture, have been fully and happily illustrated in the publications of
my learned friend, Sir William Hamilton; and it may be further observed,
that the same systematic elegance was preserved in works of a still humbler
class.   The small brass cup, of which a print is annexed (see plate III.) is
of that plain and cheap kind, which could only have been meant for the
common use of the common people.   With us, such articles, even when of
more precious materials, and more expensively decorated, are made without
any attention to symmetry of proportion, or harmony of parts:—the spout
appears to pull one way, the handle another; and an inclined top is placed
upon a flat bottom.   For as the component pieces are usually made by diffe-

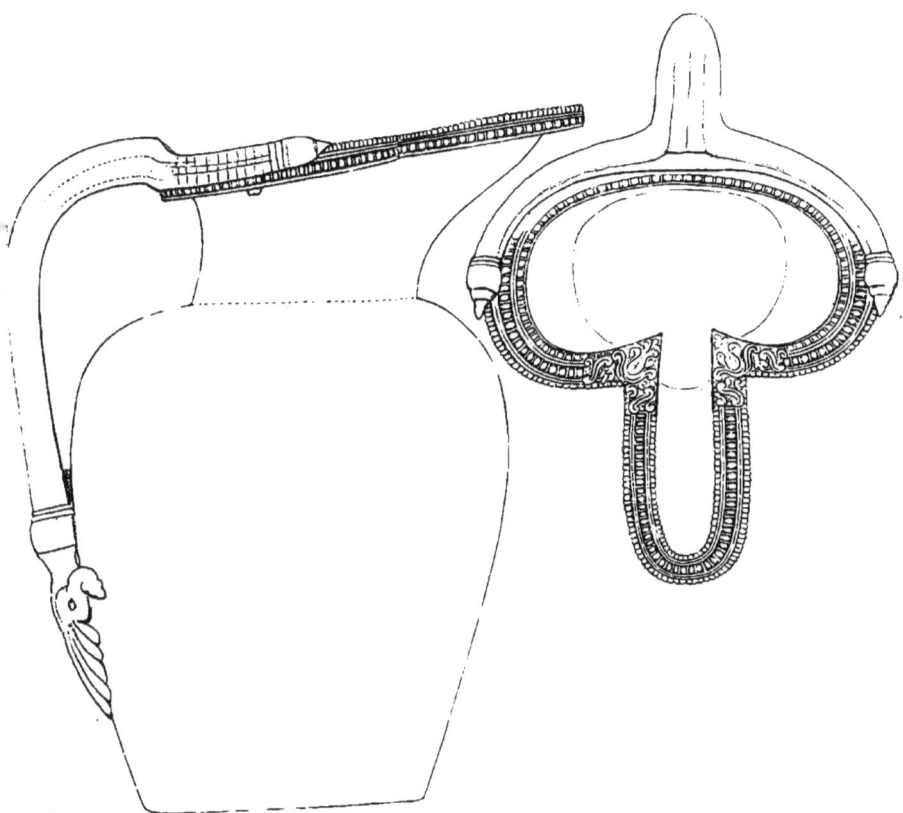

From the Original of the same size belonging to the Author.

Which through each rank of life its influence spread,
From the king's palace to the peasant's shed;
And gently moulded to its soft controul,
Each power of sympathy that moves the soul.

    Hence, every work of labour or of thought,   320
With one inherent principle was fraught;
One principle diffus'd through ev'ry part,
Alike of lib'ral or mechanic art;
From the sublime and awful grace, that shed
Its charms terrific round the thund'rer's head,   325
And the gay, sprightly elegance that shone
In the light limbs of Maia's nimble son,
Down to the humblest cup that could afford
Its scanty comforts to the peasant's board.

    In all alike we trace the same designs   330
Of just proportion, and harmonic lines;
No single part dissenting from the rest,
But all in one united form comprest.

rent hands, and put together afterwards, they have seldom any relation to
each other, except that of size.   But in the little specimen of ancient manu-
facture here given, all is in harmony and unison : the oblique line of the
bottom corresponds with that of the top; the handle bends forward in the
same direction with the spout; and all the intermediate parts are moulded
so as to have the same tendency, and an appearance of co-operating with each
other.——See plate III.

Say, why this choicest gift of fav'ring heav'n
To one peculiar people thus was giv'n?   335
Why Greeks alone, of all the human race,
E'er catch'd the vision of celestial grace;
Transfus'd it into earth's cold inert mass,
And bade it breathe in forms of ductile brass?

Was it religion, which taught men to join   340
To human figures attributes divine;
And with perfections greater than their own,
Embellish images of brass and stone?
Or was it language, whose precision taught
Conception just, and acc'racy of thought?—   345
Language, which only 'mong the Greeks was found
Complete in form, in flexion, and in sound;

v. 334. &c. Though the Egyptians and Phœnicians preceded the
Greeks in art, as well as science, they appear to have been mere manufac-
turers, wholly unacquainted with principle of grace which is here alluded
to, as the essential characteristic of liberal art. Of the Phœnicians, indeed,
we have no specimens extant, except coins, struck probably after their ac-
quaintance with the Greeks; but Egyptian sculptures are very common,
and prove that the artists of that nation ought to be ranked rather with those
of the Chinese and Hindoos, than with those of either ancient or modern
Europe. The Etruscans were merely imitators, or rather copiests of the
Greeks, as has lately been fully proved by the learned Abbé Lanzi, in a dis-
sertation on the subject.

Language, the counterpart of thought and sense,
Whose images its archetypes dispense,
And by dispensing, order and arrange,   350
Debase or elevate, preserve or change;
Whence words oft fix the features of the mind,
And stamp their character on half mankind.

 But let not language have the sole applause;
Nor yet religion seem the only cause: 355
Arise, great Homer, and assert thy claim
To ev'ry bright reward of honest fame!
From the dark gloom of undiscover'd night
Thy genius pour'd th'electric stream of light,
And wheresoe'er it beam'd, with quick'ning ray, 360
Rous'd dormant taste, and bade the soul obey;
Moulded in sound thy vivid figures rise,
Act to the ears, and speak unto the eyes:
Nature's best works in bolder models show;
Burst on the heart, and in the fancy glow,   365
 Long ere the daring Samian's plastic hand
Had taught the brass to flow at his command;

---

 v. 366. The most ancient statues in brass were composed of different
pieces hammered out, and hewn, and then rivetted together—σφυρηλατα
και σιδηροκολλητα.—At what time, where, or by whom, the art of casting
figures in metal, in moulds taken from models in clay, is uncertain: dif-

Ere Scyllis' chisel, or Dipœnus' knife,
Had hewn the stubborn marble into life,
By force intuitive thy genius felt   370
The power of art, in great Alcides' belt;
And all that after ages knew, reveal'd
In the wide orbit of Achilles' shield.

   Hence dawn'd the arts through ev'ry growing state,
And rose 'midst storms of faction, war, and hate: 375

---

ferent traditions cited by Pliny (lib. xxxv. c. 12.), gave it to Dibutades of Corinth, and Rhœcus of Samos, both of whom flourished some centuries after Homer. How far either of these traditions is true, it is not my business at present to inquire; though I may perhaps do it at some future time, if I should ever have leisure and inclination to finish a work, for which I have been long collecting materials.

   v. 368. Scyllis and Dipœnus were the first artists who were much celebrated for sculptures in marble. They flourished about the fiftieth Olympiad, or five hundred and eighty years before the Christian era; and were natives of Crete; but established their school at Sceyon.

   v. 370. See Odyss. Λ. 608, et seq.

   v. 372. See Iliad. Σ. 478, et seq.

   v. 375. Art flourished with increasing splendour from the Persian invasion to the Macedonian conquest, during one hundred and fifty years of almost uninterrupted civil wars and dissensions. By the Macedonian conquest, both the arts and literature of Greece were spread over all Asia, to the frontiers of India; and they continued to flourish under every dynasty of the conquering chiefs, till the rise of the Roman power. The

By discord fann'd, the fire of genius glow'd ;
With vict'ry brighten'd, and with conquest flow'd ;
Till Rome's benumbing influence bade it doze,
Stunn'd in the lethargy of deep repose.

coins of Mithradates are the last which display any of that greatness of style, which distinguishes those of the Greek republics, and Macedonian kings, and places them far above any subsequent works of the kind.

v. 378. A sort of miniature style became predominant under the Romans, and continued, with little variation, from Augustus to the Antonines inclusively, during a period of about two hundred and twenty years. The dissolution of all order into a military democracy, which followed the despotism of Severus, subverted even this, and left nothing but barbarism. The productions, however, of better times were still highly valued, though no longer imitated; till the establishment of Christianity, when they were beheld with abhorrence, and gradually destroyed, or buried. Constantine, indeed, for many years after his conversion, maintained universal toleration, and protected the public worship and consecrated property of the old religion from the intemperate zeal and avarice of the ministers of the new. (Euseb. in Vitæ Const. Imp. l. ii. c. 56. and 60.) But after the building of Constantinople, vanity, the leading principle of all his actions, induced him to begin the pillage of the temples, in order to decorate his new capital with such works of art, as his age could not produce ; and when he had thus broken through his own rule of moderation, he could no longer withstand the solicitations of the bishops for the utter extirpation of these retreats of the Devil, and fortresses of sin. The gold and silver statues and ornaments were consequently seized and melted; the brass carried to Constantinople; and

But short its slumbers:—see fierce bigots rise!   380
Faith in their mouths, and fury in their eyes ;
With mystic spells and charms encompass'd round,
And creeds obscure, to puzzle and confound ;
While boding prophets in hoarse notes foretell
The ripen'd vengeance of wide-gaping hell ;   385
And pledging round the chalice of their ire,
Scatter the terrors of eternal fire.

Touch'd by their breath, meek Science melts away ;
Art drooping, sinks and moulders to decay ;
Books blaze in piles, and statues shiver'd fall,   390
And one dark cloud of ruin covers all.

the marble abandoned to the destructive bigotry of the fanatic rabble (ibid.
lib. iii. c. 34 et seq.) ; by whom they were gradually broken to pieces, and the
fragments either burnt into lime, squared into blocks for building, or thrown
into lakes, morasses, and rivers.   Some were buried entire, and a few con-
cealed, by persons who wished to preserve them, in caves and cellars ; among
which was the Laocoon.   Those carried to Constantinople were gradually
melted down, as want or avarice required the materials ; but several of the
most distinguished continued in the Hippodrome, till the French and Ve-
netian Crusaders treacherously seized upon that city in the year 1204, when
they were converted into money to pay their fanatic plunderers, whom Nice-
tas Acominatus, the Byzantine historian of these events, emphatically and
justly styles ανεραςαι ϐαρϐαροι (in Excerpt. apud Fabric. Biblioth. Græc. et
Banduri Imper. Oriental.)

Much injur'd Vandals, and long slander'd Huns!
How are you wrong'd by your too thankless sons;
Of others' actions you sustain the blame,
And suffer from your darling goddess Fame: 395
For her, or plunder, your bold myriads fought,
Nor deign'd on art to cast one transient thought;
But with cold smiles of grim contempt past by
Whate'er was fashion'd but to please the eye;
The works of Glycon and Apelles view'd   400
Merely as blocks of stone, or planks of wood.
   But gloomy Bigotry, with prying eye,
Saw lurking fiends in ev'ry figure lie,
And damned heresy's prolific root
Grow strong in learning, and from science shoot; 405
Whence fir'd with vengeance and fierce zeal it rose
To quench all lights that dar'd its own oppose.

v. 408. The taste for pure and elegant composition was revived by Raphael; and expired with him. Michael Angelo was always for doing something better than *well*; and as such attempts excite the wonder and admiration of the ignorant, they are flattering to vanity, and almost certain to become fashionable; as they immediately did, both in the Roman and Florentine schools. Hence a puerile ambition for novelty and originality became the predominant principle of an imitative art, the business of which is to *copy*, and not *create*. To those, who had considered it properly, this would have

Reviv'd again, in Charles' and Leo's days,
Art dawn'd unsteady, with reflected rays;
Lost all the gen'ral principle of grace,   410
And wav'ring fancy left to take its place;
But yet, in these degen'rate days, it shone
With one perfection, e'en to Greece unknown:

appeared sufficiently difficult; since even Raphael, who excelled most in the niceties of drawing, and accurate representations of form, would scarcely have been deemed an artist by the Greeks; so very inferior are even his best performances to what remain of theirs. By *nicety of drawing and accurate representation of form,* I again repeat, that I do not mean mere anatomical accuracy in the distribution and proportion of particular parts; but that accuracy of general effect, and natural truth of gesture and expression, which alone excite sympathy, and which therefore properly distinguish *liberal* from *mechanic* imitation.

v. 112. Landscape painting was first practised by one Ludius or Lydius, in the time of Augustus, who seems to have been little better than a scene painter. Pliny says that he painted with little labour or expence, views of villas, porticoes, mountains, woods, rivers, &c. on walls (non fraudendo et Ludio divi Augusti ætate, qui primus instituit amœnissimam parietum picturam, villas et porticus, ac topiaria opera, lucos, nemoras, colles, piscinas, euripos, amnes, litora, qualia quis optarat, varias ibi obambulantium species aut navigantium, terraque villas adeuntium asellis aut vehiculis, &c. lib. xxxv. c. 10.); but that works of this sort were never held in high esteem, as pieces of art. (Idemque subdialibus maritimas urbes pingere instituit blandissimo aspectu minimoque impendio. Sed nulla gloria artificum est nisi eorum qui tabulas pinxere, &c. Ibid.) Many specimens of this kind of

Nature's aerial tints and fleeting dyes,
Old Titian first imbody'd to the eyes;   415
And taught the tree to spread its light array
In mimic colours, and on canvas play.
Next Rubens came, and catch'd in colours bright
The flick'ring flashes of celestial light;

painting have been discovered in the houses of Herculaneum and Pompeii; from which it appears, that they were rather grotesques than landscapes; and certainly very undeserving of being ranked with the ancient efforts of the art in Greece and its colonies. Glare and gaiety, however, rendered this miserable style of daubing popular among a people, who had no principles of true taste, and it served as a substitute for an art, which existed no more. With sincere regret, I observe it revived by our modern architects; for while it lasts, I fear no place will be found for the modest graces of good painting, which will naturally appear flat and insipid to eyes vitiated by tawdry and unmeaning glitter. It were well, if the opulent and magnificent of this country would be on their guard in taking the advice of builders and architects concerning the decorations of their houses; for such advisers will generally recommend the employing low artizans, in whose profits they may participate, rather than liberal artists, whose pride and spirit place them above such a base reciprocity of fraudulent traffic.

v. 415. Many of the very early painters (even the Van Eycks of the thirteenth century) endeavoured to make landscape back-grounds to their pictures; but they were rather landscapes in *form*, than in *effect*. Titian's are the first that have any pretensions to the natural graces of aerial perspective.

Dipp'd his bold pencil in the rainbow's dye,   420
And fix'd the transient radiance of the sky,
But both their merits, polish'd and refin'd
By toil and care, in patient Claude were join'd :
Nature's own pupil, fav'rite child of taste !
Whose pencil, like Lysippus' chisel, trac'd   425
Vision's nice errors, and, with feign'd neglect,
Sunk partial form in general effect.

   Hail, arts divine!—still may your solace sweet
Cheer the recesses of my calm retreat ;
And banish ev'ry mean pursuit, that dares   430
Cloud life's serene with low ambition's cares.

   Vain is the pomp of wealth : its splendid halls,
And vaulted roofs, sustain'd by marble walls.—
In beds of state pale sorrow often sighs,
Nor gets relief from gilded canopies :   435

v. 425. See note on Book I. v. 67. Claude has finished his landscapes
more elaborately than any other artist, even among the Dutch, ever did ; but
by continually working from nature, and artfully throwing in touches of apparent ease and negligence, he effectually avoided every peculiarity of manner,
and all that liny formality and smoothness, which usually results from excessive finishing. In particular forms he is often inaccurate, and sometimes
studiously indistinct, but his general effects are always perfect, and the indis-
tinctness appears to be in the medium of vision, rather than in the object seen.

But arts can still new recreation find,
To soothe the troubles of th'afflicted mind ;
Recall th'ideal worth of ancient days,
And man in his own estimation raise ;
Visions of glory to his eyes impart,   140
And cheer with conscious pride his drooping heart ;
Make him forget the little plagues that spring
From cares domestic, and in secret sting :
The glance malignant of the scornful eye ;
The peevish question, and the tart reply ;   145
The never-ending frivolous debate,
Which poisons love with all the pangs of hate :
Suspicion's lurking frown, and prying eye,
That masks its malice in love's jealousy ;
And, sprung from selfish vanity and pride,   150
Seeks, with its worst effects, its cause to hide :
Folly's pert sneer, the prejudice of sense ;
And scoffing pity's timid insolence :
Assuming bigotry's conceited pride,
That claims to be man's sole, unerring guide ;   155
Dictates in all things ;—and would e'en compell
The damn'd to go its own by-road to hell :
Officious friendship, that displays its zeal
In buzzing slanders, which e'en foes conceal ;

Kindly revives whate'er can teaze or fret, 160
Nor lets us one calamity forget;
But, tenderly, each future evil spies,
And comforts with contingent miseries:
The vapid lounger's never-ceasing prate,
Whose tiresome kindness makes us wish his hate: 465
With all the little social ills that rise
From idleness, which its own languor flies.

THE LANDSCAPE.

BOOK III.

WHAT trees may best adorn the mountain's brow,
And spread promiscuous o'er the plains below;
What, singly, lift the high-aspiring head,
Or mix'd in groups, their quiv'ring shadows shed;
What best in lofty groves may tow'r around,   5
Or sculk in underwood along the ground;
Or in low copses skirt the hillock's side,
Or form the thicket, some defect to hide;
I now inquire.——Ye woodland nymphs, arise,
And ope your secret haunts to mortal eyes!   10
Let my unhallow'd steps your seats invade,
And penetrate your undiscover'd shade.
 Ere yet the planter undertakes his toil,
Let him examine well his clime and soil;
Patient explore what best with both will suit,   15
And, rich in leaves, luxuriantly shoot.

For trees, unless in vig'rous health they rise,
Can ne'er be grateful objects to the eyes;
'Midst summer's heats, disgusted we behold
Their branches numb'd with the past winter's cold; 20
Or their thin shiv'ring heads all bristled o'er
With the dead shoots that the last autumn bore;
While their lean trunks, with bark all crack'd and dry,
Regret the comforts of a warmer sky.

Not that I'd banish from the sylvan scene 25
Each bough that is not deck'd in vivid green;
Or, like our prim improvers, cut away
Each hoary branch that verges to decay.
If years unnumber'd, or the lightning's stroke,
Have bar'd the summit of the lofty oak, 30
(Such as, to decorate some savage waste,
Salvator's flying pencil often trac'd);

v. 27. It was a maxim of the late Mr. Brown's, that every thing which indicated decay should be removed; and he accordingly destroyed in Blenheim park, and many other places, great numbers of the finest studies for art that nature ever produced. This maxim is, I believe, still followed by his successors in the trade or profession of taste; for in all the improved places that I have lately seen, I observe that the pruning goes on as unmercifully as ever; especially since Mr. Forsyth has invented a plaster, which is to produce new branches in lieu of the old ones that are cut away. Happily for picturesque beauty, I believe it does not succeed.

Entire and sacred let the ruin stand,
Nor fear the pruner's sacrilegious hand:
But premature decay offends the eye,   35
With symptoms of disease and poverty.

Choose, therefore, trees which nature's hand has sown
In proper soils, and climates of their own ;
Or such as, by experience long approv'd,
Are found adopted by the climes they lov'd: 40
All other foreign plants with caution try,
Nor aim at infinite variety.

As the quaint poets of fantastic times
Dress'd one conceit in many diff'rent rhymes,
And thought by tricks, which want of taste betray, 45
Exuberance of fancy to display ;
So the capricious planter often tries
By quaint variety to cause surprise ;

v. 43. Ariosto has concluded forty-five of his forty-six cantos with the same thought, differently expressed; and I have heard Italians cite this as a most extraordinary effort of a fertile and inventive genius; though they might just as reasonably extol the invention of an architect for making the capital of every column in an extensive building different.—Quanto diversus ab illo, qui nihil molitur inepte!—Homer, as often as he has occasion to express the same thought, always does it in the same words: this, plain sense naturally dictates; and plain sense and good taste are very nearly allied in every thing.

Collects of various trees a motley host,
Natives of ev'ry clime and ev'ry coast ;   50
Which, plac'd in chequer'd squares, alternate grow,
And forms and colours unconnected show :
Here blue Scotch firs with yellow plane trees join,
There meagre larches rise, and fringe the line ;
While scatter'd oaks and beeches sculk unseen,   55
Nor dare expose their chaste and modest green.
    O Harmony, once more from Heav'n descend !
Mould the stiff lines, and the harsh colours blend ;
Banish the formal fir's unsocial shade,
And crop th' aspiring larche's saucy head :   60
Then Britain's genius to thy aid invoke,
And spread around the rich, high-clustering oak :
King of the woods ! whose tow'ring branches trace
Each form of majesty, and line of grace;
Whose giant arms, and high-imbower'd head,   65
Deep masses round of clust'ring foliage spread,
In various shapes projecting to the view,
And cloth'd in tints of nature's richest hue ;—
Tints, that still vary with the varying year,
And with new beauties ev'ry month appear ;   70
From the bright green of the first vernal bloom,
To the deep brown of autumn's solemn gloom.

Each single tree, too, diff'ring from the rest,
And in peculiar shades of verdure drest,
Spreads a soft tinge of variegated green,   75
Diffus'd, not scatter'd, o'er the waving scene.
    Let then of oak your gen'ral masses rise,
Where'er the soil its nutriment supplies:
But if dry chalk and flints, or thirsty sand,
Compose the substance of your barren land,   80
Let the light beech its gay luxuriance shew,
And o'er the hills its brilliant verdure strew:
No tree more elegant its branches spreads;
None o'er the turf a clearer shadow sheds;
No foliage shines with more reflected lights;   85
No stem more vary'd forms and tints unites:
Now smooth, in even bark, aloft it shoots;
Now bulging swells, fantastic as its roots;
While flick'ring greens, with lightly scatter'd gray,
Blend their soft colours, and around it play.   90
    But though simplicity the mass pervade,
In groups be gay variety display'd:
Let the rich lime-tree shade the broken mound,
And the thin birch and hornbeam play around;

v. 93. Mr. Gilpin, in his Remarks on Forest Scenery, rejects the beech

Willows and alders overhang the stream, 95
And quiver in the sun's reflected beam.
Let the broad wyche your ample lawns divide,
And whittey glitter up the mountain's side ;
The hardy whittey, that o'er Cambrian snows
Beams its red glare, and in bleak winter glows : 100
Let the light ash its wanton foliage spread
Against the solemn oak's majestic head ;
And where the giant his high branches heaves,
Loose chesnuts interweave their pointed leaves ;
While tufted thorns and hazels shoot below, 105
And yews and hollies deep in shadow grow.
   Oft too, the conic fir, or round-topt pine,
In blended groups may happily combine ;

as heavy and formal; and those who judge of it from his drawings, will
probably agree with him; but if they view it in the drawings of Claude
(with whom it was a favourite tree), and then impartially examine it in nature, they will be apt to agree with me.
   v. 99. The whittey, or mountain ash, grows in the highest and coldest
situations, and is the last tree that we find in going up the Welch hills;
where the lower class of people make a thin acid kind of beverage with its red
berries fermented.
   v. 105. Hazels, yews, and hollies grow in all soils, and under the shade
of all other trees; and are therefore the best underwoods for this climate.

Or near projecting, with their sable dye
Contrast the distance, and confine the eye.　　　110
　　But, lord supreme o'er all this formal race,
The cedar claims pre-eminence of place ;
Like some great eastern king, it stands alone,
Nor lets th'ignoble crowd approach its throne,
Spreads out its haughty boughs that scorn to bend, 115
And bids its shade o'er spacious fields extend ;
While, in the compass of its wide domain,
Heav'n sheds its soft prolific show'rs in vain:
Secure and shelter'd, every subject lies ;
But, robb'd of moisture, sickens, droops, and dies. 120
　　O image apt of man's despotic pow'r!
Which guards and shelters only to devour,
Lifts high in air the splendours of its head,
And bids its radiance o'er the nations spread ;
While round its feet in silent anguish lie　　　125
Hunger, despair, and meagre misery.
　　Of all deciduous trees, that, plac'd alone,
Trust to no other merits than their own,

v. 115.　The cedar of Libanus, when old, extends its branches horizon-
tally, one over another, so as to form a kind of roof, through which scarcely
any rain can penetrate: being an evergreen, this shelter continues all the
year, so that nothing will grow under it.

The aged elm of stately growth should share,
Next to the oak and beech, the planter's care: 130
But, ah! how seldom is it seen to spread
Around the native honours of its head,
In how few instances, unmangled, bears
Th' unsully'd glories of revolving years.

   Unhappy tree! abandon'd and forlorn,   135
To northern skies from climes congenial torn;
In silent solitude condemn'd to pine,
Divorc'd for ever from its wedded vine;
And here, with mangled trunk, expos'd and bare,
Plac'd in the rigours of a wint'ry air,   140
Of all its leafy honours stripp'd and shorn,
No branches left to shelter or adorn;
A poor, blank, solitary pole it stands,
To show the naked mis'ry of the lands!

   O, all ye guardian pow'rs of beauty, rise!   145
And snatch the wretched ruin from our eyes;
Save the young brood, that yet uninjur'd stand,
And break the axe in the fell rustic's hand;

v. 155. The elm is a native of the southern parts of Europe, and never bears
seed in England; but is always propagated from layers, or cions, springing
from the roots. There are varieties of them in this country, some of which
are much superior to others, in the form and magnitude of their growth.

Or, while aloft he aims the fatal blow,
Hurl him down headlong to the fields below: 150
Call av'rice to your aid, and let it see
Its loss of profit in the stinted tree;
Count its slow growth, and tell for how much gold,
Preserv'd entire, the timber might have sold.

Next to the elm, let either chesnut claim   155
The place of honour and the crown of fame:
The one, with pointed foliage light and gay,
Op'ning its quiv'ring masses to the day;
Whilst th'other gloomy, with embow'ring leaves,
Aloft its dark and clust'ring summit heaves,   160
Or under the tall oak, extends its shade,
Excludes the sun, and deep embrowns the glade:
The one long since to classic climates known,
Has learnt the painter's mimic skill to own;

---

v. 151. The barbarous custom of shreding the elms, in hedge-rows, quite to the top, is as injurious to property as to beauty, for the growth of the tree is considerably checked, and its health injured, at every shreding; as may be seen when the trunk is cut transversely. The circles, which mark the different years' growths, will then appear of different sizes, in proportion as the tree recovered its branches; the smallest being that of the year in which it was shreded, and the largest that which preceded each shreding.

v. 161. The horse chesnut bears shade better than any other large tree.

And lightly brilliant from Salvator's hand,   165
Diffus'd its charms o'er many a distant land:
The other, in Atlantic forests born,
And yet untaught the canvas to adorn,
Demands in vain the honours of its place,
And shews in vain its venerable grace.   170
But, e'er again, should art its glories raise,
And emulate the pride of ancient days,
In Britain's happiest scenes it oft may shine,
And shew the talents of some new Poussin,

v. 165. The Spanish chesnut, of which there is great plenty in every part of Italy, seems to be the tree which Salvator Rosa chiefly studied; though he sometimes appears to have copied the beech. He never aims at variety, but generally contents himself with one sort of tree only; varied in the forms of the trunks, and distribution of the foliage, which, with his taste and invention, produce as much diversity of effect as is ever wanting in the kind of scenes which he represents.

v. 374. Nicolas Poussin's trees are still more generalized; he never, that I know of, condescending to mark the distinctive characters of any individual species. His masses of foliage, however, in their general forms and richness, have often a near resemblance to those of the American or horse chesnut, though his touch never marks the particular forms of its leaves; nor, indeed, any forms at all like them. I do not mean to insinuate that the art of painting has not lately made a great progress in those branches which have been cultivated and patronized; but since the death of Wilson, the higher style of landscape, here alluded to, has scarcely been attempted,

When gay in summer's foliage, newly drest,   175
The aged walnut shews its verdant vest,
The first distinctions it may justly claim,
And emulate th' Iberian chesnut's fame;
But short's the time its leafy beauties last;
. Down all are swept by the first wint'ry blast: 180
Then bare and desolate it spreads its arms,
Depriv'd at once of all its boasted charms;
And doom'd for many a weary month to mourn
The tedious period of their slow return.

    Poplars and sycamores alike display   185
Their foliage fall'n in premature decay;
While no grand forms of trunk or branch supply
The loss of beauties that untimely die:
But yet our planters much the poplar prize,
For its quick stately growth, and sudden size: 190
And if for gain they plant, the reason's good;
Since all they want is quantity of wood.

---

and the encouragement which he met with was not the most flattering, though his pictures have sold well since his death. In the humbler style, Morland and Ibbetson have arrived at great excellence.

    v. 179. The leaves of the walnut are among the last that appear in the spring, and the first that fall in the autumn.

But if, with beauty, they would charm the sight,
Something is more required than size and height;
Which shewn in shapes, thus formal, thin, and tall,
Make us regret they ever grew at all.　　　　196
　　The bright acacia, and the vivid plane,
The rich laburnum with its golden chain ;
And all the variegated flow'ring race,
That deck the garden, and the shrubb'ry grace,　　200
Should near to buildings, or to water grow,
Where bright reflections beam with equal glow,
And blending vivid tints with vivid light,
The whole in brilliant harmony unite:
E'en the bright flow'ret's tints will dim appear,　　205
When limpid waters foam and glitter near,
And o'er their curling crystals sparkling play
The clear reflections of meridian day ;
From buildings, too, strong refluent lights are thrown,
When the sun downward shines upon the stone ;　210
Or on the windows darts its evening rays,
And makes the glass with fire responsive blaze.
　　But better are these gaudy scenes display'd
From the high terrace or rich balustrade ;
'Midst sculptur'd founts and vases, that diffuse,　　215
In shapes fantastic, their concordant hues ;

Than on the swelling slopes of waving ground,
That now the solitary house surround.

   Curse on the shrubbery's insipid scenes!
Of tawdry fringe encircling vapid greens;   220
Where incongruities so well unite,
That nothing can by accident be right; .
Thickets that neither shade nor shelter yield;
Yet from the cooling breeze the senses shield:
Prim gravel walks, through which we winding go,
In endless serpentines that nothing show;   226
Till tir'd, I ask, *Why this eternal round?*
And the pert gard'ner says, *'Tis pleasure ground.*
This pleasure ground! astonish'd, I exclaim,
To me Moorfields as well deserve the name: 230
Nay, better; for in busy scenes at least
Some odd varieties the eye may feast,
Something more entertaining still be seen,
Than red-hot gravel, fring'd with tawdry green. ·

   O waft me hence to some neglected vale;   235
Where, shelter'd, I may court the western gale;
And 'midst the gloom which native thickets shed,
Hide from the noontide beams my aching head.

   For though in British woods no myrtles blow,
Nor rip'ning citrons in our forests glow;   240

Nor clust'ring vines extend the long festoon
From tree to tree, t'exclude the heats of noon;
Nor spicy odours, from the mountains, breathe
Their rich perfumes o'er fertile plains beneath;
Yet climbing woodbines spread their blossoms sweet,
And verdant eglantines the senses greet;   246
Wild thorns and hollies overhang the steeps,
And up the rocks the clust'ring ivy creeps.

   Then no fell scorpions point their venom'd stings;
No prowling tiger from the covert springs;   250
No scaly serpent, in vast volumes roll'd,
Darts on th'unwary loit'rer from his hold;
But fleecy flocks o'er verdant pastures stray,
And, heedless of the wolf, their gambols play;
Light o'er the mountains trip the nimble deer,   255
Nor dread the hungry lion lurking near.

   Bless'd land!—though no soft tints of pearly hue
Mellow the radiance of the morning dew,

---

v. 257. The beautiful pearly hue of the air in Italy, so happily imitated
in the pictures of Claude, arises in a great measure from the putrid vapours,
which in summer and autumn infect all the low parts of the southern provinces. To sleep in these vapours is almost certain death, especially to
a foreigner. I remember an Englishman of rank in Sicily, who treated
it as a prejudice, and in spite of every argument and persuasion that could

And melt the tender distance to the eye,
In one clear tinge of vary'd harmony :— 260
Yet guiltless autumn breathes its sultry breath,
Nor taints the breezes with contagious death ;
No fen-suck'd vapours rise, and nightly shed
Their deadly damps around the peasant's head ;
No pois'nous reptiles o'er his pillow creep, 265
Nor buzzing insects interrupt his sleep :
Secure, at noon, he snores beneath the brake,
Nor fears, diseas'd, with fev'rous pulse to wake ;
Nor e'er, at night, in restless anguish lies
Amidst the hums of pestilential flies. 270

Here no dark gulfs of subterraneous fire,
Dismay and terror through his fields inspire ;
Or bursting forth, their molten torrents pour
In blazing floods, and all his hopes devour ;

be used to the contrary, passed a night in a fisherman's hut on the borders
of the lake of Lentini; but he waked in a putrid fever, and survived only
thirty-six hours.

v. 265. Scorpions and centipedes often lurk in the mortises and holes of
old bed-posts, or the crevices of decayed floors, in the south of Europe. The
night-flies, or mosquitos, are an evil still more general, in all warm climates, and in many a most intolerable one; as whatever excludes them,
stops the free circulation of the air, and renders the heat unsufferable.

'Midst echoing shrieks of horror and affright,   275
And the dim gleams that glimmer through the night.

No earthquakes here quick desolation spread,
And show the mountains tott'ring on his head;
Or yawning chasms, that cities whole entomb
Deep in the earth's unfathomable womb.   280

Bless'd land! though vernal tempests often howl,
And winter's wat'ry clouds on summer scowl;
Yet hence our brooks in even currents flow;
Nor their parch'd beds in early autumn show;
But ever full the verdant foliage lave,   285
That hangs reflected o'er the glassy wave.

Hence too, our trees, e'en to the mountain's brow,
In full viridity of foliage grow;
Nor mourn their shrivell'd roots, and wither'd bowers,
When summer's suns exhale the vernal showers.   290

Hence, too, our pastures, rich in verdure, feed
The rising vigour of the martial steed;
With fatter juices make the milk-pail frothe,
And the meek sheep with warmer fleeces clothe.

Hail native streams, that full yet limpid glide!   295
Hail native woods, creation's boast and pride!
Your native graces let the painter's art,
And planter's skill, endeavour to impart;

Nor vainly after distant beauties roam,
Neglectful of the charms they leave at home.   300
   Let soft Hesperia's variegated coast,
Its vocal groves of pine and ilex boast ;
See, on the beach rich myrtle thickets shoot;
And orange bowers nod with golden fruit;
There, too, let mimic art employ its toil   305
To imitate the products of the soil ;
But here, on the same principle, bestow
Its skill on things which here spontaneous grow;
Nor, plac'd beneath our cool and wat'ry sky,
Attempt the glowing tints of Italy :   310
For thus compell'd in mem'ry to confide,
Or blindly follow some preceding guide,
One common beaten track it still pursues,
And crudely copies what it never views;
Manner'd and harsh, yet uniform and tame,   315
And whatsoe'er its subject, still the same.
   In ev'ry clime where heaven's all-cheering light
Succeeds alternate to the glooms of night,

v. 301.   There being no tides in the Mediterranean, thickets of myrtle overspread the sands; and gardens of orange trees often appear close to the shore. On the Roman and Tuscan coasts, too, are large woods of pine and ilex, in which the sea breezes sound with peculiar shrillness ; the thin leaf of the pine producing a sort of whistle, as it divides the currents of the air.

Some happy times or seasons will supply
Soft gleams of beauty to the painter's eye.   320
   What brilliance e'en in Belgian skies appears,
Touch'd by the silv'ry pencil of Teniers!
How clear, in Vandervelde, the seas that roll
Near to the circle of the arctic pole.
   E'en where impenetrable darkness shrouds   325
One half the year in thick cimmerian clouds;
While th'other beams upon the weary'd sight
One dazzling glare of never-ceasing light;
Through all the slow increase, and slow decay
Of the long annual night, and annual day;   330
Pale twilight glimmers grateful to the eye,
And wraps the scene in sober harmony;
While each harsh line, or glitt'ring colour fades,
Ting'd in soft hues and light transparent shades.
   Cool shades! unknown to hot meridian skies,   335
Where day and night in close succession rise,
And sudden darkness follows the last rays
That o'er the sun-burnt sands retreating blaze;
But which, on Holland's damp and marshy downs,
To Rembrandt's view display'd their mellow browns;

v. 339. Rembrandt appears to have been the first who attempted to paint the twilight, and he is certainly the last who has done it with success.

And as the cold, bare scenes his pencil trac'd,   341
With gleams of beauty cheer'd the dreary waste.
   But not in tints of air or skies alone,
Has ev'ry country blessings of its own :
Nature still just, her good and evil blends,   345
And where she errs, fancy the error mends.
No state or clime's so bad, but that the mind,
Form'd to enjoy content, content will find.
   See on Kamtschatka's ever dreary coast,
Th'alternate prey of deluge, fire, and frost,   350
The native, bury'd in his winter's grave,
Applauds the stench and darkness of the cave ;

Perhaps his drawings, which were sketched from nature, at hours when
he could no longer see to paint, express it more happily than his pictures:
though hastily executed, and without any choice of subject; he having
drawn whatever presented itself to his view, and trusted entirely to light
and shade for effect.

   v. 349.   No part of Kamtschatka will ripen wheat, and very few parts
any farinacious grain whatever.—The general food of the inhabitants is
dried fish and berries.   The country is torn by volcanos, earthquakes,
and hurricanes; and so cold, during seven months, that they live under
ground; and so wet during the other five, that they are obliged to raise
their huts upon stages of wood. The snow lies till the middle of May, even
in the low parts, from six to eight feet deep; and of course, when thawed,
produces a continued deluge, till it begins to accumulate again in October.
Yet these people assured M. Steller, that *they were the most favoured of God's*

Eats his dry'd fish with all a glutton's glee,
And thinks the bramble's fruit a luxury ;
With grateful heart his bounteous God adores,   355
Who sends the salmon yearly to his shores,
Who melts with show'rs the gath'ring piles of snow,
And bids red berries o'er the desert glow.
Of all the happiness he knows possest,
He feels no envious wish corrode his breast ;   360
While nature on his humble lot bestows
All that he wants, in plenty and repose:
Sleep lightly waves its poppies o'er his head ;
And love, with fancy'd roses, decks his bed:
Tranquil, he vegetates his life away ;   365
And knows no evil, but its swift decay.
    Still less can moral good or ill supply
Just cause for happiness or misery:
The good is oft but physical defect,
The negative result of cold neglect ;   370

creatures ; *the most fortunate and happy of beings ; and that their country was
superior to all others, affording means of gratification far beyond what were any
where else to be met with.* See Capt. King's Voyage, Book vi. c. 7.

v. 356. Vast shoals of salmon swim up all the rivers, from the middle of
May to the end of September, during which time the Kamtschadales catch
a sufficient quantity to dry for their winter's consumption. Ibid.

And partial ill, if rightly understood.
Is oft redundancy of gen'ral good.
 Even its last excess, the despot's chain,
Is oft a curb worse evils to restrain;
For few (alas, how few!) amongst us know 375
To use the blessings that from freedom flow.
 As the dull, stagnant pool, that's mantled o'er
With the green weeds of its own muddy shore,
No bright reflections on its surface shows,
Nor murm'ring surge, nor foaming ripple knows; 380
But ever peaceful, motionless, and dead,
In one smooth sheet its torpid waters spread:
So by oppression's iron hand confin'd,
In calm and peaceful torpor sleep mankind;
Unfelt the rays of genius, that inflame 385
The free-born soul, and bid it pant for fame.
 But break the mound, and let the waters flow;
Headlong and fierce their turbid currents go;
Sweep down the fences, and tear up the soil;
And roar along, 'midst havock, waste, and spoil; 390
Till spent their fury:—then their moisture feeds
The deep'ning verdure of the fertile meads;
Bids vernal flow'rs the fragrant turf adorn,
And rising juices swell the wavy corn:

So when rebellion breaks the despot's chain,   395
First wasteful ruin marks the rabble's reign;
Till tir'd their fury, and their vengeance spent,
One common int'rest bids their hearts relent;
Then temp'rate order from confusion springs,
And, fann'd by freedom, genius spreads its wings. 400

    What heart so savage, but must now deplore
The tides of blood that flow on Gallia's shore!
What eye, but drops the unavailing tear
On the mild monarch's melancholy bier!
Who weeps not o'er the damp and dreary cell,   405
Where fallen majesty is doom'd to dwell;
Where waning beauty, in the dungeon's gloom,
Feels, yet alive, the horrors of the tomb!
Of all her former state no traces left,
But e'en of nature's common needs bereft;   410
Through days of solitude, and nights of woe,
Which hopeless still in long succession flow,
She counts the moments, till the rabble's hate
Shall drag their victim to her welcome fate!

v. 405. This was written in September last, when the late most unfor-
tunate Queen of France was confined in a cell of the Conciergerie at Paris;
and though it was then very generally expected that she would be murdered;
few, I believe, imagined that her sufferings would be closed so soon.

Yet, from these horrors, future times may see   415
Just order spring, and genuine liberty:
Split into many states the power that hurl'd,
So oft, destruction o'er the affrighted world;
May hence ambition's wasteful folly cease,
And cultivate alone the happy arts of peace.   420

v. 415. The revolution that has taken place in France, is an event quite new in the history of civilized man, and therefore all conjectures concerning the ultimate consequences of it, must be vague and unsatisfactory. The expulsion of the higher orders of society by the lower frequently happened in the little republics of Greece; but those revolutions were upon too small a scale to afford any analogies, by which we may judge of the present great convulsion. In one important point only there appears a strong resemblance. It was not, as Thucydides observes, either the most numerous or most able party that prevailed, but invariably the most weak and stupid; which, conscious of its inability to contend openly for superiority, proceeded immediately to murders and proscriptions, and oppressed their adversaries before they were prepared to resist.

When the lines in the text were written, Lyons, Marseilles, and La Vendée were in a state of open rebellion against the Convention, and many other cities and provinces ready to set up the standard of revolt, if they could have been supported by any external assistance, which, to the amazement of every one not initiated into the secrets of war and government, was never granted them by any of the numerous powers that are combined to subvert the domination of their tyrants. Since that time the troops of the Convention have subdued and massacred all their opponents, and established a sort of military democratic despotism, the most tyrannical, sanguinary, and atrocious, that ever desolated the human race. The only government in history which has any resemblance to it, is that which prevailed in the Roman empire, from the reign of Septimius Severus to that of Diocletian; and which, in a period of not quite seventy years, proved fatal to more than twenty princes; reduced the population and resources of the empire to about one half of what they were before; and by destroying all taste for elegant art and polite literature, prepared the world for that great revolution in laws, manners, and religion, which soon after took place. Severus, in order to protect the sovereign power from the ambition of the provincial commanders, or the violence of the provincial armies, increased the number and pay of the prætorian guards; and instead of levying them from the peasantry of Italy, or the populace of Rome, drafted them from the bravest and stoutest of the distant legionaries; but as these drafted recruits kept up a correspondence with their former comrades, they soon became agents for the armies which they had left, and a general association of the soldiery against their sovereign and their officers took place over the whole empire, of which the prætorian camp was the centre. Corresponding clubs and committees were formed; and every commander, who endeavoured to enforce discipline, or protect the persons and properties of the provincials from violence, was hunted down as an enemy to the common cause. See Dion Cassius, lib. LXXX, who was himself in this predicament; the prætorians having demanded his head of the emperor Alexander Severus, on account of the attempts which he had made to restore discipline in the army, which he had commanded in Pannonia; and it was with great difficulty that either the authority or entreaties of that amiable prince could save him.

The armed rabble, which now govern and lay waste France, under the directions of the different clubs established in every part of that country, and concentrated in Paris, may yet proceed for many years in their career of pillage and extermination; but when depopulation and ruin are advanced to a certain extent, the constituent communities will become too thinly scattered, to hold together of their own accord, and must either divide into separate states, or submit to some external force. Even a Jacobin republic could not subsist in Siberia; and, if the present measures continue, France, in less than half a century, will become as desolate as Siberia. It is possible, nevertheless, that Paris may become a military republic, with the other departments under its control (as they now are in effect); and in that case let Europe tremble: depopulation, and diminution of internal resources, will then rather stimulate than impede conquest, as they did in Rome, which conquered the world during the most rapid decline of the population and resources of Italy; but the energy of her discipline enabled her not only to strain every sinew of her own strength, but immediately to appropriate and incorporate the strength of those whom she had exhausted her own in subduing: so that every conquest became the means of another. Should the excessive rigour, and sanguinary severity of the present government in France become systematic and permanent, and take a military turn, it will be formidable indeed, and endanger the very existence of civilized society; for among nations, as among individuals, those who hold their own existence in contempt, have the existence of others at their command. Polybius says that a Roman soldier never quitted his post, because he was sure to be punished with death if he did; and we learn from several atrocious instances, that the number of the offenders never gave an individual a chance of escaping; many hundreds being often put to death at a time. The French seem at present to be as little susceptible of any *compunctious visitings of nature* as the Romans were; and when there is no alternative but victory between a bullet and the guillotine, their soldiers will be apt to prefer the chance of the former to the certainty of the latter; and, consequently, to fight with extreme obstinacy and ferocity.

As far as a mere observer may venture to form an opinion concerning the measures of ministers and generals, whose circumstances and situations he cannot possibly understand, the present war, as it has been hitherto conducted, is exactly calculated to produce this effect; and consequently to co-operate with the views of the sanguinary rulers of Paris, who excited it. By not avowing their intentions, the allied powers with-hold all security from the well-disposed among the French, as to what may be the consequence of their success; whether a mere restitution of order, a division into separate independent states, or a partition among themselves; and it cannot be denied that both the late transactions in Poland, and the points to which they direct their attacks, strongly favour the last supposition; which, if prevalent in France, must ever consolidate the bulk of the nation against them, in spite of all the calamities suffered from internal tyranny. Individuals, however, might be induced to purchase their own safety by delivering up the towns and armies, with which they are intrusted by their sanguinary and capricious despots; but, unfortunately, the treatment which La Fayette, Dumourier, &c. have experienced, will effectually deter any one from following their examples; for when the only alternatives are the *certainty* of a dungeon in Germany on one side, or the *probability* of the guillotine at Paris on the other, every man who has either sense or courage will, without hesitation, prefer the latter.

When a thief once complained of the hardship and injustice of being hanged for stealing a horse of small value, the worthy judge who condemned him observed, *that he was not to be hanged for stealing a horse, but to prevent horses from being stolen.* Happy would it be for mankind, if this excellent observation were to guide the decisions of all who have the power to punish. In the instance above cited it is exactly reversed: a poor fugitive being punished by the most rigorous imprisonment, not to prevent others from imitating his crimes (for the whole nation was previously implicated), but to deter them from participating in his repentance, and force them on in the career of their wickedness. Even the author of evil is said to incite men by transient pleasures to the commission of those sins, for which he afterwards eternally torments them; but to enforce damnation by pains and penalties, and thus to make destruction at once the means and the end, shows a degree of refined malignity, which neither faith nor fiction have yet ventured to attribute to the Devil.

From this instance of private passion triumphing over public policy, there is but too much reason to apprehend that it will do so in others; and that we shall see a sordid lust of dominion, and a paltry ambition of extending their frontiers, influencing the conduct of princes, at a moment when their thrones are sinking under them, and the whole fabric of civil society is tottering round them: let them however remember, before it is too late, that if one side makes the war, a war of *kings*, the other will make it a war of *peoples*; and in such a contest, the *many* will prevail every where against the *few*; but let them make it (what it really is, and ought solely to be) a war of civilization and order, against barbarism and anarchy, and every man who values the blessings of civilization and order, will go heart and hand with them. Direct force will, nevertheless, be found inadequate to repel the overwhelming weight of the torrent, unless means be found to divide the current, and make one part of it counteract the other. Had there been one great statesman employed in Europe, this must have been done before now; but the race of great statesmen seems to be either extinct or out of fashion; and instead of them, we have now crowds of courtiers, sophists, and declaimers, whose talents bear the same proportion to those of great statesmen, as the accomplishments of a good drill serjeant to those of an able general.

B. I. l. 146. *for* painted *read* pointed.

www.ingramcontent.com/pod-product-compliance
Lightning Source LLC
Chambersburg PA
CBHW021424090426
42742CB00009B/1241